40 Alternatives
to College
James Altucher

CONTENTS

Dedication

To everyone who has taught me ever since the day I finally escaped the educational system.

Why Don't Send Your Kids To College?

I have two messages. One for kids and one for parents.
FOR KIDS:
You're worthless. That's what they are telling you. If you don't go to college you will "ruin your life". You will "not have a job". You will "be a [name the worst possible job you can imagine here]". We'll get more into it later. How you will have the most amazing life you can possibly imagine.

But let's first look at their agendas. And when I say they, I mean: your friends, your parents, colleges, the government, future bosses. They all have agendas that have nothing to do with you being smarter, more social, or happier.

You friends want you to go to college because they are going to college, so they want to rationalize their decisions.

Your parents want you to go to college because they have their own feelings of worthlessness and are projecting that onto you. Why else would they want to force you to go hundreds of thousands of dollars into debt to somehow "have the life they never had." And I'm not being critical of them. I love your parents. They raised you. They got you to this point. We'll deal with them in a bit. Don't worry about them.

Colleges of course want you go to college. College tuition has gone up 10 times since 1977. Inflation has gone up 3 times. Healthcare has gone up 5 times. We had a national debate about healthcare a year or so ago. But no national debate about tuition costs despite it being one of the most important life decisions you will ever make and you are being forced at gunpoint to make it at such a tender age.

Your future bosses. They think they are worthless also. But what gave them a tiny ounce of worth was that they have a piece of paper on their wall that says they spent four years drinking and screwing around and getting in debt and more or less surviving. So they want some justification that their decisions were correct. So who are they going to hire: the person who helps them feel good about themselves for about half a micro-second, or you – who calls into question all of their feelings about self-worth, about existence itself.

The US Government. Why would they care if you go to college? Student loan debt is now higher than a trillion for the first time. Student loan debt is now higher than credit card debt for the first time. Student loan debt is BACKED by the US Government. Who makes money when you go to college? The US Government. Get yourself into indentured servitude. They don't care!

Wow! That's a lot of people, institutions, and governments you have to take care of. And you're only 18. I feel for you. Don't worry. We're going to make it better.

FOR PARENTS:

Please, for god's sake, ask yourself these questions:

A)   Do I want to go into taking on my child's debt after he graduates college? Because you might have to.

B)   Do I want to go into debt by promising my kid college when he doesn't want to go into debt?

C)   The average student takes five years to go to college. That's a long time. We don't know how long we will live. That's a big chunk of our lifespan. And your kids have already spent 12 years sitting at desks, taking tests, being around kids of the same ethno-demographic. Do they really need another four years of that? Is that such a great thing?

D)   I ask you: name me, really, ten things you learned in college? Now, name me 3 things you actually used after college in your jobs?

E)   Finally, wouldn't it be great if your kid can have a better education, have a better time, maybe make more money, be in less debt, make more friends, make more connections, develop more skills, become more mature, and all the time you save more money? This is not a dream question asked by a genie. This is reality. This is a real question because it can and should happen.

Let's do a little FAQ (frequently asked questions). I got a lot of hate mail after I first started writing that our children shouldn't go to college. You can imagine. I got death threats even. And it was quite annoying. I don't like getting death threats. I get scared. But it shows me that what is touching on a core fabric of our society. The American religion that says "kids must get a college education". And I got a lot of questions:

Q: *James, you went to college. So how can you tell your kids not to?*

A: It's precisely because I went to college that I am most qualified. None of my jobs afterwards made use of anything I learned in college. My professors were boring and none of them were people I wanted to look up to or mentor me. And I saw exactly what was going on in college while thousands of kids parents were paying up to $40k (now $70k) a year when you include room, board, books, travel, etc.

Q: *What about the statistic that was PROVEN in study after study that kids who went to college make more money 20 years later than their counterparts that did not go to college?*

A: First off: the study is completely fake and anyone who took Statistics 101 in college knows that but I'll get to that in a second.

Think about 20 years ago. College was cheaper. There weren't as many reasons NOT to go. And there weren't as many alternatives as they are now.

So what did smart, ambitious kids do? They went to college. What did kids who did not feel as ambitious do? They didn't go to college.

So the study has what is called "Selection Bias". They assumed they had one audience in their group that they were testing (people who went to college) but, in fact, they really had a completely different group (smart, ambitious kids versus not-as-ambitious kids).

A true test would be to take 2000 kids accepted by a wide variety of colleges. Then say to half the kids, "You can NEVER go to college". And then 20 years see who made more income. My guess is the group that did not go to college.

How come?

Because they would have a five year head start. They would not be required to study a bunch of classes they didn't want to take in the first place and would never remember, and they would have the enormous gift of not having to be perhaps hundreds of thousands of dollars in debt. Or even tens of thousands of dollars in debt is still too much for a 23 year old.

I'm going to give you forty alternatives to college. They are all going to be exciting and wonderful opportunities where my criteria were:

- You learn.
- You make friends.
- You learn about life.
- You get a head start on learning what you might be passionate about.
- For the first time you experience things you never experienced before and would perhaps never get the chance to experience again.

- You spend less money than college would've cost you.
- You learn things that were never taught in college (and I'll describe first what those items are since they are extremely important in being successful later on. Better to learn them early than later).

So What, Then, is My Agenda in Writing This?

People have been through a lot this past decade. The economy has fallen apart. The future has abruptly changed for both parents and young children and yet the student loan debt crisis has grown larger. My agenda is that I want people to have less stress.

I want the new generation of young people to be just as creative and innovative as prior generations. I charge the minimum price Amazon will allow me on this book (99 cents) but it's free if you are in Amazon's "Prime Member" program. I want people to be less stressed, I want society to be better, and I want to be happy seeing all the inventions of the next generation in line for the success this country has always promised.

The TRUE COSTS of College

First, let's look at something that every kid learns in Economics 101. Opportunity Cost: If you spent 5 years spending on average 50k a year then your true cost is not $50k. It's $50k + what you would have made if you did not go to college. Let's say you could've made $20k. Then your true cost of college is $70k a year. But let's dive into this a bit further.

The average tuition cost is approximately $16,000 per year. Plus assume another $10,000 in living costs, books, etc. $26,000 in total for a complete cost of $130,000 in a 5 year period (remember, across the country the average amount of years spent in college is five years). In fact, according to the Department of Education, over 54% of students graduate in six years or more. But we will assume the average.

Some people choose to go more expensive by going to a private college and some people choose to go a little cheaper by going public but this is an average. Funny enough, Georgetown University mentioned me specifically and criticized my numbers. They neglected to mention they cost $70,000 per year. But I don't hold grudges.

Over the course of a lifetime, according to CollegeBoard, a college graduate can be expected to earn $800,000 more than his counterpart that didn't go to college. $800,000 is a big spread and it could potentially separate the haves from the have-nots. But who has and who doesn't?

If I took that $130,000 and I chose to invest it in a savings account that had interest income of 5% per year I'd end up with an extra $1.4 million dollars over a 50 year period. A full $600,000 more. That $600,000 is a lot of extra money an 18 year old could look forward to in her retirement. I also think the $800,000 quoted above is too high. Right now most motivated kids who have the interest and resources to go to college think it's the only way to go if they want a good job. If those same kids decided to not go to college my guess is they would quickly close the gap on that $800,000 spread.

The reason I can make this calculation is because if you don't go to college you can start saving immediately. When will the college graduates start to save? When they are 30? 40? 50? When will they have their student loans paid off given that student loans are at the highest level ever? We have no idea. We have never experienced this before.

Many people wrote me and said, "I paid back my student loans right away." Fine, you went to school 50 years ago! We have NEVER EXPERIENCED the situation we are in right now.

Student loans are a national crisis. A national shame. Let's examine some of the reasons why people say kids should go to college and we will unveil the fallacies.

10 Reasons People Say Kids Should Go To College

1. People say: Kids learn to be socialized at college. Are you kidding me? I'm going to spend $100-200k a year so my kids can learn how to make friends with other people their age? Let me tell you about how your kids will be socialized in college and you know this to be true:
—-Your kid should put a dime in a glass jar every time he or she has sex in his first year of college. After the first year of college, he or she should take a dime out every time they have sex. They will never empty that jar. I might be exaggerating but I'm not far off. So assume that's step #1 on the socialization of our children in college.
——Do the same exercise above with the dimes but replace "sex" with "vomit". That's part #2 with the socialization.

——You can also do the above exercise with the dimes (give your kid lots of dimes before they say, "ok, Dad, see you LATER!" when you drop them off in the parking lot of college.) but instead of "sex" or "vomit" say "classes I will skip because of either sex or vomiting."

2. People say: Kids learn how to think in college. This argument was said to me by Kathryn Schulz, author of "Being Wrong", a good friend and author of an excellent book. But she knows more than anyone that no matter how much you think you "think", you're also going to be wrong most of the time. And by the way, does it really cost several hundred thousand dollars to learn how to think? Does "think" have a price tag on it.

I would argue that college is a way to avoid learning how to think. If I want to learn how to play tennis, the best thing to do is go out on a tennis court and play tennis. If I want to learn how to drive a car, I better get behind a wheel and drive. If I want to learn how to live and how to think, then the best thing to do is begin living my life and thinking my thoughts instead of still having my parents pay for my life and my professors giving me my thoughts. See below to see how I learned how to "think".

3. Statistics say: College graduates make much more money than non-college graduates. See my analysis above.

4. One person said: Not everything boils down to money. Specifically, one brilliant commenter on one of my posts said, "I'd say the overwhelming majority of people don't go to college as a financial investment. They do it because they want to explore career options in an easy environment. They do it because there's a particular career they want to be (unfortunately weekend hackers don't often become doctors). They do it because they want to drink and party on the weekends. They do it because the point of life is not making money."

I'm going to be angry for the first time in this book. What a stupid statement that is. If it's not a financial investment then why has the cost of college gone up 1000% in the same amount of time it has taken healthcare to go up 700% and inflation to go up 300%? It's a financial investment because college presidents have scammed most kids into thinking they can't get jobs without college. So they jack up the prices knowing kids will be forced to pay otherwise suffer the perceived opportunity cost of not going to college.

Also, the commenter above says "the point of life is not making money". I'd like to thank him for saying that. Otherwise I would've gone through life thinking the entire point of life was making money. I'm assuming what he really means by that statement is that it's great for kids to read books about philosophy, literature, art, history, etc. in an environment that encourages discussion among peers and experts. This is what college is truly great for. But if people, young or old, are interested in reading something – they will read it. Else, they won't.

5. My Experience: I think of myself as an educated person so let me tell you my own experience:

College itself was spent:

Meeting and fooling around with girls for the first time in my life. I'm glad the banks loaned me enough money to do this. And fortunately, extreme failure, lots of apologies, and embarrassment in this arena didn't affect me at all later in life.

Learning about alcohol and the occasional recreational drug for the first time in my life.

I took an enormous amount of classes in Computer Science. None of which helped me in my first actual non-academic job. In fact, I was so bad at computers after going to both undergrad Cornell in Computer Science and graduate school at Carnegie Mellon in Computer Science that my first non-academic job (HBO) had to send me to two months of training courses at AT&T so I could learn a thing or two about how computers were used in the real world. My first task at HBO was to get some computer they gave me "onto the Internet". I ended up crashing the computer so bad they had to throw it out and I also wiped out everyone's email on that computer. I thought they were going to fire me but they just banished me for two months instead. The only way to get fired at HBO, I was told, was to stand on your boss's desk and pee on it.

I borrowed every penny of my college education. I took courses every summer (they were cheaper and quicker then) and I took six courses a semester. I still graduated without about 30-40k in loans. It took me ten years (and selling a business) but I paid back every penny of my loans.

On top of my courses, I worked about 40 hours a week at jobs so I could afford my expenses. My parents did not pay one dime of my expenses except for maybe my first semester of college. And for graduate school I got a full scholarship and stipend.

The way I got educated in reading, philosophy, history, art, etc. was fully on my own time. After leaving graduate school I took relatively easy jobs as a programmer on campus. I spent hours every day reading books, and then at least another hour or two a day going to the campus library and reading criticism on the books I had just finished.

Why so late? Why did I wait until then? Who knows the mysteries of the human heart? It wasn't until I was 25 that I really fell in love with reading. And then I read everything I could.

And this reading was the entirety of my liberal arts education. And it was all for free and has served me well since then. And I was actually paid while I was doing it. I would say I've made more money from this free education I put myself through than anything I learned in school.

If you can't read a book without being on a college campus and paying $100-200k a year for the honor of being there then you probably shouldn't be reading books anyway. Or at least wait until you learn the value of a dollar before making that extreme expense.

6. Parents are scammed. If you are a parent and wish to send your kids to a college then, just to summarize, here is what you are paying for:

Your kids are going to have sex 1- 5 times a day with people you probably wouldn't approve of.

Your kids are going to drink, smoke pot, probably try LSD and other drugs before you even get back home after dropping them at the dorm.

Your kids are going to cheat on most of their exams. When I first started college I wanted to be a psychologist. I read every book on psychology. In Psych 101 I got a D- on my first exam, which was graded on a curve. Apparently the other 2000 kids in the class had access to older exams which were stored at all the fraternities and the professor never changed the exams. I had to ultimately drop Psych as a major. My dad said, "Why do you want to major in Psychology anyway. Girls won't like you because you won't make any money as a psychologist." I said, "but then I'll never know if the girls like me for money or not?" And he said, "Girls won't like you because you have money. They'll like you because YOU ARE THE KIND OF GUY who can make a lot of money."

Your kids are going to make connections with other like-minded individuals (people focused on drugs, socialism, sex 24 hours a day (not a bad thing), people cheating on exams, and people with rich parents who will help your kids get jobs at Goldman Sachs).

Your kids are going to think they are smarter than you almost immediately.

While you are working 60 hours a week and borrowing money to send your kids to college, your kids will be sleeping good chunks of the day, relaxing on the weekends, and enjoying the blissful pleasures of the lazy life for another four years until the real world hits.

And by the way, I know my title said "10 Reasons" and I only listed "6". I didn't learn to count in college. But maybe you can help me fill out three more reasons in the reviews for this book. I had a great time in college. And although I worked very hard I managed to enjoy the beautiful nature around Ithaca and really appreciate being away from home. I graduated a year early so I could save on tuition. In order to graduate early I had to maintain at least a 3.0 average. Unfortunately, on the last day of classes I realized I was heading for a 2.999 and would not be able to graduate. I had to go to my Fortran (blech!) professor and beg him to upgrade me from a D+ and a C-. Fortunately, he did. And I got my degree.

So what, then, is my agenda in writing this? People have been through a lot this past decade. The economy has fallen apart. The future has abrubtly changed for both parents and young children and yet the student loan debt crisis has grown larger. My agenda is that I want people to have less stress. I want the new generation of young people to be just as creative and innovative as prior generations. I am not making any money at all on this book. I want people to be less stressed, society to be better, and I want to be happy seeing all the inventions of the next generation in line for the success this country has always promised.

Questions People Ask Me About The No-College Stand

When you say that parents should not send their kids to college, do you mean that they should not go to college indefinitely? Or come back to college later in life?
Kids at 18 have no idea what they want to do in life. The world is a very big place. It's bigger than five classes a day on philosophy or chemical engineering. Most kids at 18 don't relish philosophy but they relish the experience of freedom and being out of their parents' home for the first time in their lives. There is nothing wrong with this. Young adults have a lot of energy and should use it. But the problem is that college costs have risen 1000% in the past 30 years while healthcare has risen 700% and inflation has risen "only" 300%. Colleges have made use of the myth that you can't get a job unless you have a college education. So young people feel a rush to get that college out of the way so they can get a job and "begin" their adult lives. I think kids should begin their adult lives at 18 by experiencing what else the world has to offer other than a classroom (which they've all just been locked in for the prior 18 years). A rose needs space to bloom.
Then, later, if they've thought about the debt burden they will place themselves and their parents in, they can choose to go to college. Right now student loan debt is greater than homeowner debt and credit card debt in this country. That's a lot of debt. Whereas previously we've created generations of innovators and creators, now we are creating a generation of young people mired down in hopeless debt. When will they get to live life?
When did you come up with your theory? How did you come to think of your theory?

A lot of people say, "Oh, James Altucher went to college so he shouldn't be talking about this". Well, why not? I saw what people were doing in college. I know now how much I learned in college and how much I learned in other experiences in life and which is more relevant to me now at the age of 43. And, by the way, it was much cheaper when I went to school than it is now. So when did I develop this theory? Almost immediately when I realized college had nothing to do with any successes or failures that I had in life (and I had A LOT of failure despite college). And also, it took my 8 years to pay back my student loan debt. Now it takes kids 30 years to pay down that debt. It's not fair to the youth of our country. To summarize:

A) You learn very little that you use in real life.

B) You are so burdened by debt that you can't use your new-found knowledge to create real freedom and joy for yourself.

C) A young person can use their energy in many other ways than just college.

Do you think that nothing well worth learning is taught in college? Or is it the fact that students might not be willing to learn?

There are many things worth learning in college. And not every person in the world should avoid college. But the best colleges cost a lot of money and it's a burden for young people. And most things that you can learn in college you can learn for free outside of college thanks to the Internet. For instance, computer programming is best learned on the job. English literature is best learned by reading the books you are passionate about. Writing is best learned by having real experiences, writing every day, and reading the great writers who inspire you. Philosophy is learned by having real experiences and reading the philosophers or religious practitioners who inspire you. Imagine learning all of these things because of real world experiences, and then not having any debt. Also, when learning is not force-fed, you develop a real love and knowledge for how to learn on your own and that's something you keep for the rest of your life. Most young people don't learn this.

Do you think you learned anything when you went to college? Or do you think you could have learned more if you chose not to go to college?

I went to college from 1986-1989. I was paying for it with debt so I graduated in 3 years. I took six courses a semester so I could graduate early. And I took courses every summer. I also worked about 30-40 hours a week at jobs so I could afford my expenses outside of tuition. Even then I graduated with enormous debt. I majored in Computer Science and learned how to program. I thought I was a very good programmer when I graduated college. I prided myself into thinking I was the best since I was sure I was better than any of my classmates.

While I was in college I programmed computers to play chess, I wrote papers that were published in international conferences on artificial intelligence, I got As in every practical programming-related class (other than Fortran, ugh!), and then, by the way, I got a full scholarship to go to graduate school for two years. Then, when I finally had a job in the "real world" my programming awful! I was still nowhere near ready to do real world programming. It probably took about another six months of daily effort to learn how to really program. I had the passion for computers and I'm sure if all I had done were those AT&T courses right from the beginning I would've been fine.

Sometimes you have to throw a kid in the water to teach them how to swim (or let them drown). That's the way to learn. Not being force-fed from textbooks written twenty years ago and being taught by professors with little real world experience. It's a shame also that unless you have a PhD a college won't let you teach (in most cases). PhDs are often the most intellectual but have the least real world experience. And for that great experience we have to go into massive debt now.

Do you have any advice for students who are in college right now and feel like they aren't getting anything out of their education?

Yes, take a year or two off and try some of my alternatives.

Are there many people who disagree with your thoughts? How do people react when they first hear what you have to say?

I think many people agree and don't say anything. But the people who disagree get very upset. It's like I'm questioning their religion. I can go right now in the center of Times Square in NYC and shout, "Jesus is Satan!" and people would just walk around me and think, "ok, it's free speech". But if I shouted, "don't send your kids to college", WHOAH!! Lock this guy up! Take away his kids! People have a huge life attachment to the fact that college is a part of life, the same way that birth, marriage, parenting, and death are. It's not. It's a relatively modern invention (for the mainstream American, it's about fifty years old the idea that most kids should go to college, after 6000 years of civilization).

Unfortunately this modern invention has been so abused by college administrators that the next generation of kids we graduate will be mired down in debt, and STILL need to learn the skills required for basic jobs that they want to do. Let's not forget, nobody learns how to be a doctor in college. That's pre-med. They learn a little in one or two years of medical school, but then they really learn when they are a resident in an actual hospital. And then between debt, insurance, and the burdens government is now placing on doctors, how will they ever pay down their obligations? The entire system needs to change but the discussion has to happen somewhere. Hopefully it will be here.

Anything else you would like to add?

I began my career at the age of 23, after I left graduate school. And then I began a career from scratch again when I was 26, and then 28, and a totally new career when I was 33. And then a completely new career when I was 36. And now I'm 43 and I'm still open to changing careers and doing new things in life. There's no rush to start a career at the age of 22. Life changes as you go out in the world and experience things. Failures happen; seeds grow and take years to turn into a tree. Give yourself time to plant those seeds, to learn from your failures, to experience new things in life. The earlier you start to do this, the wiser, healthier, and more balanced you will be. You will be more capable of making decisions on career, family, and life in general.

Don't discount the value of spending time experiencing the world before you make the enormous financial commitment of going to college. It will teach you the beginnings (and JUST the beginnings) of what might be important to you. It will teach you how to survive, it will teach you about people other than from your own age group and socio-economic demographic, it will teach you about the 99% of opportunities that happen in the world that have nothing to do with college, it will teach you how to stretch your mind to learn how to sell and communicate, and finally it will show you at an early age that failure, choices, and life is a spectrum and not a ladder. Take advantage of that when still young and I can guarantee you all of life will bend down and support your endeavors.

Note: this has nothing to do with money. This has to do with making the most out of your life.

Didn't your own kid say to you: "people who go to college have better jobs 20 years later"?

When my kids quote me a statistic like that it sounds to me like they are being coerced into going to college. Someone is trying to make a 12 year old afraid that something bad will happen to them if they don't go to college. So then out of six years of brainwashing and fear tactics they make their decision.

But anybody who takes Statistics 101 in college knows that the stat they quoted me includes very basic selection bias. As I mentioned, the real test is to take 2000 people who want to go to college. I.e. they have ambition, drive, intelligence, etc. Divide them in half. Tell one half they can go to college. Tell the other half they can't EVER go to college. THEN see where they are in 20 years.

My guess is the side that had a 5 year head start (on average it takes 5 years to complete a 4 year degree) and was not saddled with $100-300k in debt is far ahead of the side that went to college for five years (and then perhaps graduate school afterwards).

Does anyone learn anything in college?

Let me ask you a couple of quick questions. At some point you came across these facts in either college or high school. See if you can answer quickly and correctly without looking it up. They are very simple: When was Charlemagne born? Name the different types of clouds? Who was William Mckinley's Vice-President?

Does Google care about your college education?

Actually, they do. I know one guy whose company was being acquired by Google and they asked for his SAT scores. However, when you interview for a job at Google here are some sample questions (and the idea is: your college education will not help you answer them): How many bottles of shampoo are produced around the world in a year? How many ridges are on the rim of a quarter? Design an evacuation plan for San Francisco? How many tennis balls can fit in this room? What comes next in the following series: SSS, SSC, C, SC

The idea is that a college education will fill your memory. Teach you a lot of facts. Maybe teach you basic analysis that conforms to your teacher's opinions. But will NOT teach you how to really think. Will not teach you how to come up with ideas. How to sell ideas. How to be creative. How to navigate through interesting experiences so you won't get hurt.

I tell my kids: I will let you do whatever you want in the world EXCEPT for college at the age of 18. Take some time before you spend $200k on something when you don't even know what you want out of life yet.

Let's not forget that high school and below are primarily advanced babysitting services. So what makes college different? You're still with the same demographic of people. You still have homework and tests and memorization of facts. The only difference is now you (most likely) live on your own. Is college the safest environment to do that? Is that the wisest use of the highest tuition costs ever? I doubt it.

Learn how to learn. Then go wherever in the world you want to go. Because the world will be yours.

10 Things I <u>Didn't</u> Learn in College

1.- HOW TO PROGRAM COMPUTERS

I spent $100,000 of my own money (via debt, which I paid back in full) majoring in Computer Science. I then went to graduate school in computer science. I then remained in an academic environment for several years doing various computer programming jobs. Finally I hit the real world. I got a job in corporate America. Everyone congratulated me where I worked, "you're going to the real world," they said. I was never so happy. I called my friends in NYC, "money is falling from trees here," they said. I looked for apartments in Hoboken. I looked at my girlfriend with a new feeling of gratefulness – we were going to break up once I moved. I knew it.

In other words, like was going to be great. My mom even told me, "You're going to shine at your new job."

Only one problem, as you already know, is that when I arrived at the job, after 8 years of learning how to program in an academic environment – I couldn't program. I had no clue. I couldn't even turn on a computer. It was a mess. I think I even ruined people's lives while trying to do my job. I heard my boss whisper to his boss's boss, "I don't know what we're going to do with him, he has no skills." And what is worse is that I was in a cluster of cubicles so everyone around me could here that whisper also.

So they sent me to remedial programming courses in New Jersey. If you've never been in an AT&T complex it's like being a storm trooper learning how to go to the bathroom in the Death Star where, inconceivably, in six Star Wars movies there are no evidence of any bathrooms.

Seriously, you couldn't find a bathroom in these places. They were mammoth but if you turn down a random corner then, Voila! – There might be an arts & crafts show. The next corner would have a display of patents, like "how to eliminate static on a phone line – 1947". But I did finally learn how to program.

I know this because I ran into a guy I used to work with ten years ago who works at the same place I used to work at. "Man," he says, "they still use your code." And I was like, "really?" "Yeah," he said, "because it's like spaghetti and nobody can figure out how to modify it or even replace it."

So, everything I dedicated my academic career to was flushed down the toilet. The last time I programmed a

computer was 1999. It didn't work. So I gave up.
Goodbye C++. I hope I never see you and your "objects" again.

2- HOW TO BE BETRAYED

A girlfriend about 20 years ago wrote in her diary. "I wish James would just die. That would make this so much easier. Whenever I kiss him I'm thinking of X". Where X was a good friend of mine. Of course I put up with it. We went out for several more months. It's just a diary, right? She didn't really mean it! I mean, c'mon. Who would think about someone else when kissing my beautiful face? I confronted her of course. She said, "Why would you read through my personal items?" Which was true! Why would I? Don't have I have any personal items through my own I could read through? Or a good book, for instance, to take up my time and educate myself? Kiss, kiss, kiss.

Why can't they have a good college course called BETRAYAL 101. I can teach it. Topics we will cover: Betrayal by a business partner, betrayal by investors, betrayal by a girlfriend (I'd bring in a special lecturer to talk about betrayal by men, kind of like how Gwynneth Paltrow does it in Glee), betrayal by children (since they cleverly push the boundaries right at the limit of betrayal and you have to know when to recognize that they've stepped over the line, betrayal by friends/family (note to all the friends/family that think I am talking about them, I AM NOT – this is a serious academic proposal about what needs to be taught in college) – you help them, then get betrayed – how to deal with that?

Then there are the more subtle issues on betrayal – self-sabotage. How you can make enough money to live forever and then repeatedly find yourself in soup kitchens, licking envelopes, attending 12 step meetings, taking medications, and finally reaching some sort of spiritual recognition that it all doesn't matter until the next time you sink even lower. This might be in BETRAYAL

201. Or graduate level studies. I don't know. Maybe the Department of Defense needs to give me a grant to work on this since that's who funds much of our education.

3.- HOW TO WRITE

Oh shoot, I was going to put Self-Sabotage into a third category and not make it a sub-category of How to Be Betrayed. Hmmm, how do I write myself out of this conundrum? College, after all, does teach one how to put ideas into a cohesive "report" that is handed in and graded. Did I form my thesis, argue it correctly, conclude correctly, and not diverge into things like "Kim Kardashian will never be the betrayer, only the betrayed? And this brings me to: Writing. Why can't college teach people how to actually write? Some of my best friends tell me college taught them how to think. Thinking has a $200,000 price tag apparently and there is no room left over for good writing.

And what is good writing? It's not an opinion. It's not a rant. Or a thesis with logical steps, a deep cavern underneath, beautiful horizons and mountaintops at the top. It's blood. It's Carrie-style blood. Where everyone has been fooling you until that exact moment when now, with the psychic power of the written word, you spray pig blood everywhere, at everyone, and most of all you are covered in blood yourself, the same blood that pushed you and your placenta out of your mother's womb, pushed and shot out with you until just the act of writing itself is a birth, a separation between the old you and the new you – the you that can no longer take the words back, the words that now must live and breathe and mature and either make something of themselves in life, or remain one of the little blips that reminds us of how small we really are in an infinite universe.

4.- DINNER PARTIES

How come I never learned about dinner parties in college. Sure, there were parties among other people who looked like me and talked like me and thought like me – other college students of my age and rough background. But Dinner Parties as an adult are a whole new beast. There are drinks and snacks beforehand where small talk has to disguise itself as big talk and then there's the parts where you KNOW that everyone is equally worried about what people think about them but that still doesn't help at those moments when you talk and you wonder what did people think of ME? Nobody cares, you tell yourself, intellectually raffling through pages of self-help books in your mind that told you that nobody gives a **** about you.

But still, why don't we have a class where there's Dinner Party after Dinner Party and you learn how to talk at the right moments, say smart things, be quiet at the right moments, and learn to excuse yourself during the mingling so you can drift from person to person. Learn how to interrupt a conversation without being rude. Learn how to thank the host so you can be invited to the next party. And so on. Which brings me to:

5. NETWORKING

Did it really take 20 years after I graduated college before someone wrote a book, "Never Eat Alone?" Why didn't Jesus write that book? Or Plato? Then we might've read it in religious school or it would've been one of those "big Thinkers" we need to read in college so we can learn how to think. I still don't know how to network properly so this paragraph is small.

I'm classified under the DSM VI as a "social shut-in". I'd like to get out and be social but when the moment comes, I can only make it out the door about 1 in ten times. I always say, "I'd love to get together" but then I don't know how to do it. Perhaps because not one dollar of my $100,000 spent on not learning how to program a computer was also not spent on learning how to network with people

6. Politics. My very first girlfriend, the girl who first laughed hysterically when I showed her a piece of chewing gum I found on the ground that had sculpted itself into the muddy shape of a heart, took me to a movie called "Salvador". Then there was a discussion group afterwards about how the Contras are bad, or good, I forget, and everyone was nodding and speaking in a Spanish accent. And afterwards my girlfriend was upset, "why aren't you talking?" because truth was I was so tired I couldn't think, but nobody ever taught me how to tell the truth so I lied and said, "it moved me so much I'm still absorbing it" and my girlfriend said, "yeah, I can see that." And nobody ever taught me that there's more than one acceptable opinion on a college campus.

My roommate for instance would tell me, "Reagan is definitely getting impeached THIS TIME." And I visited his dad's mansion over Christmas break and he told me all about Trotskyism and the proletariat and I had to work jobs 40 hours a week while taking six courses so I could A) graduate early and B) pay my personal expenses and when I would run into him he had long hair and would nod about how a lot of the college workers (but not the lowest-paid, poorest treated ones – the students who worked) were thinking of unionizing and he was helping with that. "Do you have a job?" I asked and he said, "no time". And that's politics in college.

What about the real politics of how people try to backstab you at the corporate workplace or VCs never properly explained the "ratchet" concept to you before they kicked you out of the company and then re-financed. Nobody told me a thing about that in three years of college and two years of graduate school. I wish I would've known that for my $100,000.

7. FAILURE

Goes without saying they don't teach you this. If you are going to pay $100,000, why would you fail? You might think you were wasting your money if the first mandatory elective you had to take was about failure. About wondering how you were going to feed your family after you got fired when something that was not your fault: Post-Traumatic-Lehman-Stress Syndrome, a common medical condition coming up in the DSM VII.

8. SALES

When I was busy learning how to "not program" nobody ever taught me how to sell what it was I was programming. Or sell myself. Or sell out. Or sell my ideas and turn them into money. Or sell a product to someone who might need it. Or even better, sell it to someone who doesn't need it. Some business programs might have courses on salesmanship but those are BS because everyone automatically gets As in MBA programs so that the schools can demonstrate what good jobs their students get so they then get more applicants and the scam/cycle continues. But sales: how to demonstrate passion behind an idea you had, you built, you signed up for, so that people are willing to pay hard-earned after-tax money for it, is the number one key to any success and I have never seen it taught (properly) in college.

9. NEGOTIATION

You've gotten the idea, you executed, you made the sale and now…what's the price. What part of your body will be amputated in exchange for infinite wisdom? Will you give up one eye? Or your virility? Because something has to go if you are up against a good negotiator.

What? You thought (like most people without any experience do) that you were ALREADY a good negotiator. Let me tell you, a good negotiator will skin your back, tattoo it with "SUCKA" and hang it up above the fireplace in his pool house if you don't know what you are doing.

The funny thing is, the best sales people (who are just aiming for people to say "YES!") are often the worst negotiators ("it's very hard to say "No" when you are trying to get people to "Yes"). These are things I wish I had learned in school. I've been beaten in negotiations on at least 5 different occasions, which fortunately became five valuable lessons I've learned the hard way, instead of studying examples and being forced to think about it for the $100k in debt I got going to college. People will say, "Well, that's your experience in college. Mine was very different." And it's true. You joined the sororities and learned how to network and dinner party and be political and everything there is to know about betrayal. My college experience was sadly unique and probably different from everyone else's so you would be completely right to quote me that inane statistic about how college graduates earn 4% more than high school graduates and are consequently 4% happier (another thing, 10. HAPPINESS. We never learn how it's a combination of the food we eat, our health, our ability to be creative, our ability to have sound emotional relationships, our ability to find something bigger than ourselves and our egos to give up our spiritual virginity to.)

So I can tell you what I wish I did. I wish I had gone to Soviet Russia, and played chess, and then gone to India and learned yoga and health, and I wish I had gone to South America and volunteered for kids with no arms, and did any number of things. But people then say, "ha-ha! But that cost money." And they would be right. It would cost less than $100,000+ but would still cost some money. I have no idea how much.

But one of these days when the scars of college go away and I truly learn how to think. I might have better comebacks for these people. Or if I truly learn, I would learn not to care at all.

If Your Kid Insists He/She Wants To Go to College

Give them the facts and give them options. Tell them how much debt they will incur. Let them know the truth. Teach them about money responsibility and have them think for themselves if it will be worth their future debt. See if this in itself can turn into a lesson in money management. A first experience of what the real world is made of.

Talk with them about the alternatives. The entire world is open to them. It's the most exciting thing in the world. If they can get free of the brainwashing put on by guidance counselors, the government, their friends, the colleges, then they can truly break free.

They can begin to live a unique life, a special life that will allow them to quickly rise above the forest and see all the trees, a life not weighed down by the stresses of debt, and how quickly they can get promotions and raises in a dead-end career where there is no safety anyway.

They can become themselves, and the beautiful beings they were meant to be.

40 Alternatives to College

1- START A BUSINESS

Before I describe this I want to answer the first two questions that immediately come up: a) not everyone is meant to be an entrepreneur. I agree with that. Failure is a horrible thing. But we all face it in one form or other throughout our lives. There's nothing wrong with an 18 year old failing and learning to get through that. But being an entrepreneur will teach you how to form ideas, how to sell those ideas to investors, customers, and employees (if you have any), and will teach you a lot about managing limited resources such as money and labor. It will also teach you about negotiation, about execution, and many of the things I mentioned above are not taught in college.

This is the college of the streets. And when you have to eat what you kill, you learn extremely fast.

b) Doesn't it cost money to start a business? Yes. But it's much less than the money it costs to go to college and the costs of starting a business are going down precisely when the costs of going to college are going up. My last business, Stockpickr, I started for $2500 and I probably could've started it for less. I made many times my investment on that. And that was five years ago. It would be cheaper to do now. The Internet has leveled the playing field.

Again, on the "not every kid is Bill Gates" point. Of course that's a true statement. But there's no law against being an entrepreneur. In fact, everyone can be an entrepreneur. You don't need a degree for it. So what they really mean is: "not everyone can be a successful entrepreneur". And as far as I know, there's no law against failure either. When someone loses a tennis match or a chess game, how do they improve? They study their loss. As anyone who has mastered any field in life knows: studying your losses is infinitely more valuable than studying your wins. I failed at my first three attempts at being an entrepreneur before I finally learned how to spell it and I finally had a success (i.e. a company with profits that I was then able to sell).

To summarize:

Failure is a part of life. Better to learn it at 18 than at 23 or older when you've been coddled by ivory blankets and hypnotized into thinking success was yours for the taking.

Get baptized in the river of failure as a youth so you can blossom in entrepreneurial blessings as an adult.

What do you learn when you are young and start a business (regardless of success or failure)?

You learn how to come up with ideas that will be accepted by other people. Most kids graduate college with an atrophied idea muscle. Starting a business forces you to exercise that muscle every day.

You begin to build your b/s detector (something that definitely does not happen in college).

You learn how to sell your idea.

You learn how to build and execute on an idea.

You meet and socialize with other people in your space. They might not all be the same age but, let's face it, that's life as an adult. You just spent 18 years with kids your age. Grow up!

You might learn how to delegate and manage people.

You learn how to eat what you kill, a skill also not learned by college-goers.

2- TRAVEL THE WORLD

Here's a basic assignment. Take $10,000 and get yourself to India. Check out a world completely different from our own. Do it for a year. You will meet other foreigners traveling. You will learn what poverty is. You will learn the value of how to stretch a dollar.

You will often be in situations where you need to learn how to survive despite the odds being against you. If you're going to throw up you might as well do it from dysentery than from drinking too much at a frat party.

You will learn a little bit more about eastern religions compared with the western religions you grew up with. You will learn you aren't the center of the universe. Knock yourself out.

3- CREATE ART

Spend a year learning how to paint. Or how to play a musical instrument. Make a band and tour with it. Or

write 5 novels. Learn to discipline yourself to create. Creation doesn't happen from inspiration. It happens from perspiration, discipline, and passion. Creativity doesn't come from God. It's a muscle that you need to learn to build. Why not build it while your brain is still creating new neurons at a breathtaking rate than learning it when you are older (and for many people, too late).
I didn't write a novel in college. But I did attempt four novels in my 20s. Did I publish them? No. Did I make a lot of money from them? No. But I learned how to write. And I learned it for free and on my own time while I was working full time jobs.
I put in my 10,000 hours writing at a relatively early age. And that virtual apprenticeship has made me a considerable amount of money since then. And I didn't need college to do it. In fact, college got in the way of starting earlier.

4- MAKE PEOPLE LAUGH

This is the hardest of all. Spend a year learning how to do standup-comedy in front of people. This will teach you how to write. How to communicate. How to sell yourself. How to deal with people who hate you. How to deal with the psychology of failure on a daily basis. And, of course, how to make people laugh. All of these items will help you later in life much more than Philosophy 101 will. And, by the way, you might even get paid along the way.

5.- WRITE A BOOK

Believe me, whatever book you write at the age of 18 is probably going to be no good. But do it anyway. Write a novel about what you are doing instead of going to college. You'll learn how to observe people. Writing is a meditation on life. You'll live each day, interpret it, and write it. What a great education!

6.- WORK IN CHARITY

Plenty of charities do not require you to have a college degree. What is going to serve you better in life: taking

French Literature 101 or spending a year delivering meals to senior citizens with Alzheimers, or curing malaria in Africa. I have an answer to this. You might have a different one. And, by the way, if you do any of these items for a year, two years, maybe ten, then maybe go to college? Why not? It's your life.

7.- MASTER A GAME

What's your favorite game? Ping pong? Chess? Poker? Learning how to master a game is incredibly hard. Let's start with the basics:

Study current experts on the game. Videos, books, magazines, etc. Replay, or try to imitate in some way, the current masters of the game.

Play a lot: with friends, in tournaments, at local clubs, etc. Take lessons from someone who has already mastered the game. This helps you to avoid bad habits and gets someone to immediately criticize your current skills. Mastering a game builds discipline lets you socialize with other people of all ages and backgrounds but who have similar passions, and helps you to develop the instincts of a killer without having to kill anyone. Nice!

Once you master one game, it teaches you "how to master" in general. This is an incredibly useful skill to learn. Particularly if you can do it for cheap. A chessboard and some chess books cost a lot less than a college education.

8.- MASTER A SPORT

Probably even better than mastering a game because it's the same as all of the above but you also get in shape. I look back at myself: I imagine what if I had gone to India and spent a year learning yoga. Amazing! I would've made friends from all over the world, I would've gotten in shape, I would've been fit and healthy. I almost can't write these words. It's so sad for me to see the opportunities I've missed.

9.- WANT TO BE A DOCTOR? Don't you need a degree? Maybe.

But first, how many bad doctors are out there? People with no bedside manners. No compassion. They hear your symptoms, listen to your heartbeat, and then turn to a big reference book to figure out what anti-biotic you need. And, by the way, they overprescribe highly dangerous anti-biotics just to not take any chance. I can do that!

So before you sign up for ten years of hell and a million in debt do this: Volunteer at a hospital, or at a morgue, get in touch with your element, see what they do, how they work, you may find doctors don't quite know as much as you thought they did, you may find you don't like being vomited on. You may find you don't like changing bed pans. You may find that you weren't as compassionate for this type of life as you thought.

See if you may like to explore Chinese medicine instead which looks at the body in a different way than western medicine and has different costs in training. I'm not making a judgment on which is better. But take your time before making a decision that will change your life forever at the age of 18.

10.- WANT TO BE A LAWYER?

Work as a paralegal, do it for free for a year, see what really goes on in the law firm. Watch those lawyers working 80 hours a week, sleeping in the office. See the first year associates come in with their huge debts to pay only to find themselves in caucus rooms full of boxes with boring documents that they have to highlight for at least a year or two. See if you want that.

If you truly like legal work there are many ways you can do it without a degree. For instance, set up websites that help people get access to legal advice for cheap. You don't want to give the advice yourself (because of the scam of legal education, it's against the law) but you can provide pointers to the basic templates for wills, partnership agreements, divorces, etc. so that people no longer need to spend tens of thousands of dollars on these documents by using lawyers that charge $500 an hour to just fill in some blanks.

Be smart about it. If you love the law, there's 100 ways to get involved without having to be a lawyer. But first work as an intern in a law firm and see what it's all about.

11.- DO ANYTHING YOU WANT FOR ONE YEAR

You've just worked pretty damn hard from the ages of 4 to 18. Take a break. Go swimming. Lower your expectations about what you need to accomplish so quickly. In the past 100 years lifespans have more than doubled. There's no rush at the age of 18 to dive into five more years of stress.

Take a break. It's when you lower your expectations that the full range of possibilities becomes open to you. Try it and see what happens, what passions fall your way.

12.- GO TO UNCOLLEGE.ORG

Take courses in things you are interested in. The web is an amazing thing. They didn't have it when I began college. But there are sites like uncollege.org where you can see a full list of courses being offered online but universities from all over the world. From Stanford to MIT to random courses on just about any topic.

Why not "study" at uncollege.com for free (or cheap, as some of the course cost) and see what really interests you?

Here are some of the college courses offered at uncollege.com:

Stanford Artificial Intelligence Course. Free online course with 140,000+ participants at Stanford.

MIT Open Course Ware. Follow the curriculum guides to get a free MIT education. Various multimedia and resources for each course.

The Open University. 600+ free online classes with exercises. Track progress. Use forum. Intro to advanced classes.

UC Irvine OCW. 190 UC Irvine courses.

OCW Consortium. For more Open CourseWare universities, see current members, including 22 U.S. universities and many from around the world. The search engine for finding courses is mediocre.

Harvard Med School OCWI. 115+ Harvard Medical School courses.

Open Yale Courses. 30+ Yale courses, all subjects. Available video and audio are on iTunes and Youtube.

Stanford Engineering Everywhere. 13 Stanford engineering courses.

There are also thousands of courses listed that aren't from the traditional courses but could be even more valuable.

For instance, here is a sample list:

Google Code University. Google courses for coding, programming. It's Google so it has to be good.

Udemy. Attend or create online courses. From free to $250 on any subject. Can include video, PowerPoint, PDFs, audio, and or classes.

Learnable. Attend or create online courses from $10-50 on Web Dev, Tech, Lifestyle, and Business.

TED. Tech Entertainment Design. Presentations of the most innovative ideas from around the world.

Academic Earth. Lecture videos from the best universities in the U.S. Thematically organized into playlists. Also organized by subject and by university.

Khan Academy. 2,400 videos and some practice exercises. Lots of math, some science, some finance, test prep.

13- DO THE DAILY PRACTICE FOR A YEAR AND SEE WHERE IT TAKES YOU

The basic idea is to kick start your health, your idea muscle, your creativity, your motivations, and your spiritual life. The body is not just your muscles and blood and bones. But it's also your emotions, your brain, your mind, and your ability to give up control over every aspect of the world. All of these things must work in conjunction to live a healthy, happy, and successful life. For example, if negative people keep trashing your ideas, insulting you, and dragging you down, then you must consciously move away from them. Not as easy as it sounds and is part of the emotional aspect of the daily practice.

I built a site (to use it is totally free) that allows you to check the boxes each day on the Daily Practice. Not necessarily to measure progress. The key is not to be competing with yourself every day. The key is to be happy. This is what worked for me and still does. And progress is individual for each person.

The basic default goals I put up there are:

PHYSICAL:
Exercise
How Many Hours Did You Sleep?
What Did You Eat Today?

EMOTIONAL:
What Negative People Did you ignore
What People Did you Connect?
What positive people did you bring into your life?

MENTAL:
Idea List (with functionality so people can track ideas)
What Did You Read Today (not counting media)

SPIRITUAL:
What am I grateful for today?
What spiritual practice did I do today?

These are just starting points. For instance, for myself under "Mental" I put: "Books I am reading today" so I can keep track over time what books I've read (or started).

I've seen over the past 20 years and from probably over 1000 testimonials now, that persistent use of the Daily Practice as a guiding principle (regardless of religion, creed, race, etc.) has a tendency to completely change one's life every six months. I've seen it with me and I continue to see it.

14- TAKE A JOB

Yeah, that's right. Why wait until 23 when you are $200k in debt. Take one now when you are $0 in debt and see what happens. Doesn't matter where. Be the janitor at a McDonalds. You'll learn how to work. You'll learn about customer satisfaction. You'll be forced to deal with people who are not like you (and you might not even like). These are skills not taught in college and many people learn them too late in life.

Not only that, a job has two other benefits:

A)   You can rise up and make a lot of money.

B)   You can see where the gaps are in an industry, which will give you ideas on how to start a business. There's also the benefit, of course, where you will have money.

15- WRITE A SCRIPT FOR A MOVIE

Go ahead, try it. You won't be able to do it later. Watch a bunch of horror movies and then write a script for one. Get Syd Field's book on writing screenplays. It might be a crazy idea. When you are 40! But it's certainly not a crazy idea right now.

16- DIRECT A DOCUMENTARY ON SOMETHING YOU ARE INTERESTED IN

For instance, do you like baseball? Track down everyone who has caught the baseballs of record-breaking hits: Babe Ruth's homerun record, Hank Aaron, Derek Jeter's hitting record, etc. I'm making this up off the top of my head. I hate baseball. But a documentary like this has a nice arc: with each segment, for instance: what made Ruth such a success, or Aaron, or whoever. Why was the baseball so coveted? Follow its rise in price over the years and see who owns it now and why. Baseballs like this are religious icons in America. Following their path is pure iconography. It's perfect for documentaries.

Or, if you want to get a documentary on HBO: interview all the prostitutes and call girls in your suburb. Anything goes when you are doing a documentary! And, even better, you can do the whole thing on your cell phone! You have to love the Internet and the advances in technology in the past 30 years.

17- AUDITION IN BROADWAY FOR A WHOLE YEAR

See what it takes, how you can do it. Acting is not a bad skill to learn no matter where your life takes you. And you will build friendships and contacts from all walks of life. And you never know, you could be a star!

18- VOLUNTEER GARDENING AROUND YORU NEIGHBROHOOD

You will learn about real estate, about gardens and plants. Shovel snow in the winter. You will learn about your community.

19- BECOME A REAL ESTATE AGENT

See if you have what it takes to sell things. Real estate is probably about to boom no matter what I write about why I personally would never want to own a home again.

Let's look at a basic fact: there are 300mm people in America. Eventually, there will be 350mm people. That's 50mm extra houses needed. Why can't you make money right now selling them? You will learn marketing, sales, interior design, the basics of architecture, and again you never know who you can meet in the process of this that could catapult your career in a completely different direction.

20- TAKE UP YOGA

And I don't just mean the physical aspects. Yoga is a way of life that cleanses the body. It's about nutrition. It's about being honest. It's about meditation. It's about being kind to people. And, getting back to the physical, you will get into BRUTAL shape. Is that such a bad thing to do for a year than spending $50000 going to a school?

Oh, and by the way, if you did yoga for a year you'd probably be able to start teaching it and making some money. And learning how to teach, how to explain basic concepts, how to overcome shyness, are valuable tools not taught in school. Not to mention you might find a business to start: maybe a new kind of yoga clothing.

21- GO TO 4 VIPASSANA MEDITATION RETERATS WITHIN ONE YEAR

They are completely free and brutal. Get to see how your mind works. Vipassana, which means "seeing things as they are", is a style of meditation that requires intense sitting and diving into the mind. Observing what it does to you. It's completely free and there are centers all over the world. A retreat takes ten days. You will learn more in those ten days about your mind and your body than you can learn in six months of college.

22- STUDY WHATEVER IT IS YOU ARE INTERESTED IN. GET IN THE GAME

My two daughters are interested in manga comic books, which is a multi-million dollar industry in Japan. They draw manga characters all the time and come up with stories for them. They know every style. They've read books on manga drawing. They've read hundreds of manga books.

I would love to give them the opportunity to spend a year studying it at a very deep level. To attempt to master the art. They already know more than any college student about manga drawing. Imagine if I could give them the chance to become among the best in the world at it. Which is what would happen if that was a direction they would choose. For me, it doesn't matter. But for them, it could be their dreams come true.

23- BECOME A CONNECTOR, MAKE THINGS HAPPEN

You might say, "Well don't I have to be already big in an industry to connect people". Here is what you do: get someone who is an expert in a field you are interested in to agree to give a talk. Let's say it's about entrepreneurship. Get a law firm to sponsor it (they would love to – think of all the potential clients in the audience) and use Facebook to market the event. BAM! You'll meet a million people. Get everyone in the audience to sign up on an email list. Then hold networking dinners, etc.

Your personal network has real value. Networking does happen in college but it is 1/10 the networking you can do on your own.

24) BECOME A PARTY PLANNER

Sweet 16s, Bar Mitzvahs, Weddings. Figure out all the people in your area that offer services for parties. Then offer to organize events for cheap. You can be cheaper than any other planner out there because your personal expenses are cheaper. And, again, the networking you develop will be invaluable. Not to mention: parties are fun.

25- LEARN AND MASTER A FOREIGN LANGUAGE

Include a trip at the six month mark so you will see if you are really learning it. I took French for five years in high school and college. I cannot speak to you one word of French. The way to learn a language is to intensely study it 5-7 hours a day and then go to that country and speak it. And you will learn it.

Don't learn French, though. Time to either learn Chinese or Portuguese (Brazil).

26- GRAB WHATEVER IT IS THAT IS BUGGING YOU, BOTHERING YOU, UPSETTING YOU, AND SOLVE THE PROBLEM.

Are charities wasting too much money on salaries? Do research; write an article, do a blog, a documentary, expose the problem.

Here's another idea for you: there's a lot of class action lawsuits in this country. Make a website that is a central resource for these. Do lead generation then for the law firms. You can make a lot of money this way. And help a lot of people.

27- BECOME A PERSONALITY

Write articles for all websites that will let you syndicate your work. Just to give you an example: when you are 18 you obviously know all the stars and celebrities that 17 year olds love. Make a blog, syndicate it, write about every piece of news on these celebrities, capture all their twitter feeds, photos, etc.

I'm not suggesting you become a Perez Hilton or a paparazzi. Find something you're interested in, and build a website that makes you the central source about that topic.

This teaches you how to build a website. How to do research in the real world (as opposed to research about Oliver Cromwell or whatever you are studying in college), how to distribute your ideas, how to become a better writer and communicator, etc. And maybe you make some money out of it. Worse things have happened. I know a 17 year old making $5000 a week profit off of his website and just decided not to go to college.

28- WRITE AND PITCH YOUR OWN TV SHOW

TV is not dead as a medium. In fact, it might be just beginning with Hulu and Netflix starting to offer original programming plus 500 cable channels that need new programming.

Every day come up with 10 ideas for TV shows and how you would shoot them. Before you finish your first year of doing this you will have at least several good ideas you can go ahead and shoot.

What if you like an existing show? Write a spec script for them and send it in. Hollywood TV studios bring in writers all the time who submit spec scripts. It's very hard and it's very competitive but you're 18. You have time.

29- GO TO MOTIVATIONAL SEMINARS

In every city there are motivational seminars you can attend. You don't have to spend $5000 to attend a Tony Robbins seminar but you can spend much less and get just as much value from any number of speakers who have been successful in life and now want to transmit that success to you.

That's valuable information they will be imparting. Imagine year learning from these mentors. Do your research, make sure they are good, put in the time to ensure the message is one that resonates with you and that the teachers have integrity, and then go for it. Learn.

30) PLAY!

You are off school and 18 for crying out loud! Go canoeing, hiking, anything.

When I was 4 years old and about to go off to nursery school for the first time, my dad told me: "first there's nursery school, then kindergarten, then grades one through twelve, then graduate school, then a job for forty years, then you can retire."

WHAT!? I think I started to cry. I liked my life JUST AS IT WAS. I wanted to play. Well, now you can again. You don't have to be 65. You can be 18. And then at 19 figure things out.

31- BECOME A MODEL OF WHATEVER YOUR SIZE IS

You are beautiful no matter who you are or what you look like. Learn the fashion industry. Work in it. Intern in it. Pose for it. Wear a bracelet and have those pictures appear in a pamphlet. There's nothing wrong with trying.

32- GO TO SAN FRANCISCO AND MINGLE WITH SILICON VALLEY

No matter what people say, if you want to do a tech startup, go out to San Francisco, go to the tech meetups, learn who the movers and shakers are, learn how to code, and start a business.

Your networking ability there is 1000 times what it would be in Kansas City. That's why Google started there. That's why Facebook moved out there. That's why Apple is there. That's why you can be there. And by the way, Steve Jobs didn't get a college degree. Nor did Bill Gates or Larry Ellison (the CEO of Oracle).

33- VISIT ALL THE ARCHITECTURAL HISTORIC SITES OF EUROPE.

You want history? You don't need to spend $200,000 in college learning it. Go to HISTORY. Go to all the places. Learn the lessons learned on those very spots. Think about them. Study them. You will survive on your wits. You will become more of a world citizen than any young person stuck on a 3 square mile college campus in the middle of nowhere.

34- BACK PACK EL CAMINO THE SANTIAGO – THE WAY OF ST. JAMES

Thousands of spiritual seekers a year hike this trail in Spain. Paulo Coehlo has written books about it. Many people have said it has changed their lives. Before you rush head first into the crushing world of materialism give yourself a chance to experience what a spiritual quest might look like. You can experience it a little bit by reading *The Alchemist* by Coehlo but what if you can actually experience it.

35- HIKE THE APPALACHIAN TRAIL

Similar reasons as above. But you learn how to survive on your own, in the woods, without a soul in sight. You may never get this chance again to confront your fears, your sense of self-worth, and your loneliness.

36- MAKE YOUR OWN LIST OF ALTERNATIVES

Make your own list of alternatives that really resonate with you. This is my list of what I think will work for young people. Add to it. And email me at altucher@gmail.com and give me more alternatives. I'll put up a post when I get enough alternatives. Again, this is about exercising your idea muscle. It's really hard. It's just as hard as exercising your physical muscles. My brain hurts writing this. I'm sweating.

37- VIRTUAL MENTORS

I still do this. A few weeks ago I watched every Woody Allen movie. I read his books. I read every interview he did. I wrote a blog post: Nine things I learned from Woody Allen. Because I spend so much time trying to get to the essence of his work and art, my efforts were appreciated and the article proved to be enormously profitable.

Every week I study a new virtual mentor. Right now I'm studying the life of Howard Hughes. I've also been studying the life of Gandhi. These are people who changed the world. Who created things. People who mastered the fields they found themselves in. Who created entire new worlds from the visions in their mind. Did they go to college? Gandhi did (he was a lawyer by training). But Howard Hughes didn't and re-created the oil industry, the movie industry, the aviation industry, and Las Vegas.

38- RUN FOR OFFICE

This might seem like a joke. You're only 18. But run for city council. Or run for mayor. Become familiar with all the issues in your town. Come up with a platform about how your town can be improved. Part of your campaign is that you have no financial incentive for what you are doing. And then run for office.

This will teach you how to speak. Again, how to come up with ideas. How to communicate them. How to allocate resources. How the political power system works.

And guess what? You'll probably lose. Like Margaret Thatcher did on her first campaign for office at age 24. Like Bill Clinton did on his second campaign for governor. Like Winston Churchill did repeatedly. But losing is part of life. Then you come back. Then you become perhaps the greatest politician ever and really do something that can change our lives.

39) Raise funds for a cause you feel strong about,
Use kickstarter, for instance, to raise the money. Make a difference.

By the way, who are you raising funds from? Rich people. Successful people. People you can learn from. People you can later ask advice from. People who will remember you because they will say, "this is an 18 year old who cared". Guess what? There are not that many 18 year olds who care. Now you can be one of the few.

40- WATCH A MOVIE A DAY FOR A YEAR
There's a book about this. A boy didn't want to go to college so his father said, "fine but on one condition. Watch one movie with me every day." The boy agreed. They talked about each movie. He learned from it. And his relationship with his father changed every day. That year changed his life. If you don't want to watch a movie every day read one book a week that you and one of your parents pick and discuss it at the end of the week. Movies are about life. They are about pain. They are often about the troubles of adulthood. What a better education then to watch these movies and discuss them with an adult who has maybe been through some of these issues.

I miss my father. He's dead now for six years. I wish he had made an offer like that to me when I was 18. He was very busy working and couldn't do it. But now I miss him.

Conclusion

I could've made this list 100 alternatives long. But I think you should come up with alternatives as well. There's lots of ways to get experience, learn skills, make money, avoid debt, find happiness, avoid sadness, and deal with the fear that you aren't accomplishing something simply because you didn't choose the too-easy path of going to college at the age of 18.

Debt is very stressful. It crushes lives. It turns people with every opportunity in front of them into indentured servants. It prevents you from following your passions. It prevents you from changing the world.

Give yourself a chance. Give your parents a chance. At least spend a year trying the above alternatives or one of your design. Maybe spend two, or even three. Heck, maybe spend the rest of your life doing one of the above. I'm sure if you do that you will make the world a better place. And when that happens, everyone who goes to college will benefit from the smart choices you made.

Articles

Other Books By James Altucher

How To Be The Luckiest Person Alive!
I Was Blind But Now I See
The Altucher Confidential (the first blog to become a
comic book!)
FAQ ME

About the Author

James Altucher has failed at numerous business and careers and succeeded at a few of them. He has loved and lost and loved again. He has tried over and over to… [insert just about anything from chess to poker to hula hooping to massive lifestyle experimentation]. He has won success and lost it and occasionally wins it again. Has been on a quest for the meaning of happiness since the age of six (only because before that, happiness was fairly easy and simple). He has written nine prior books including "I Was Blind But Now I See".

James writes at JamesAltucher.com the most personal, embarrassing stuff a person can possibly write. He tweets @jaltucher.

Made in the USA
San Bernardino, CA
01 October 2016